# unbosoming

unbosoming
Written by Samridhi Prakash
Paperback Edition

First Published in India in 2022
by Inkfeathers Publishing, New Delhi 110095

Copyright © Samridhi Prakash 2022



www.inkfeathers.com

# unbosoming

samridhi prakash

Inkfeathers Publishing

www.inkfeathers.com

for baba
hope you were here
to stroll through these myriad thoughts
and sort siestas from nightmares

"i thought how unpleasant it is to be locked out;
and i thought how it is worse,
perhaps, to be locked in."

virginia woolf

# praise for the book

"A remarkable effort and achievement.
The writing is both timeless and worth reading immediately."

**-Aisha Ghani, Happiness & High Performance Coach**

'unbosoming' is a beautiful collection of poems by Samridhi Prakash, where her judicious choice of words, poetic cadence and powerfully curated images conjoin to paint a world of lived experiences. Her poems have thematic variations that speak of love, longings, alienation but there is a distinct structural unity, which keeps the readers mesmerized. Here is a poetic world carved out of private and public spaces meeting and intersecting each other with a glistening of emotions and tenderness of feelings. Her words seem to be soaked with passionate thoughts. Her poetic vision lends to her experiences and deep meditation on things.

There is a conscious presence of the past in her poems rendered with honesty of intent and purity of thought. Samridhi is a new voice in Indian English poetry endowed with new sensibility.

**-Prof. Chandra Shekhar Dubey, Poet, Writer, Critic and Researcher**

# gratitude

This piece of me is for every human/non-human whose life force collided with mine. I felt you, I hurt you, I learned from you, I remembered you. All of you made me dream. unbosoming was born out of our shared stories, and I am forever grateful to our fates and destinies for intersecting, even if for the briefest of human seconds.

Lavanya, my editor, and Shivani & Ansh, my interior illustrators. Your creative minds brought life to my emotions. There are not enough words to express my gratitude. I dreamt of unbosoming and you guys already had it by the time I woke up.

The one person I am forever indebted to, my mumma. You have been my strength and my constant friend at every crossing. I admire your resilience, your values, and your capacity to love. Thank you for believing in me when no one did, thank you for reading the never-ending poetry I used to write as a kid and not laughing, thank you for not scolding when I used to scribble lines at the back of my copy instead of studying, thank you for reading Tinkle to me every night and for every second of your love. Thank you for bringing me down here despite every difficulty. You make me so much more. Thank you to the man who worked hard day and night to give me a better life. I saw you little as a kid, but I see you now. I see you, papa and I respect you. Thank you for making me a better human and breathing your values in me. Thank you to my foundation stones, my brothers, Satwik and Shubhrak. You taught me how to fight, how to be brave, how to bluff, how to tie my shoes, how to swing, how to play football and every other sport, how to chew gum, how to annoy the life out of a person, how to always be there for the other. You have been my favourite teachers. Thank you for loving me the way you do. I am grateful to my entire family, every individual, every relation. All of you have qualities I look up to, I learn from. Dadi, your stories remind me to be bold and badi ma, your smile gives me hope to brave on, and nana-nani, your secret smiles have revealed to me the colours of love and to every other member, you have taught me so much and for which I am so grateful. And oh, my forever favourites, Vaibhavi and Siddharth. Your support keeps me sane, and your faith keeps me going. I would give up my happiness for yours in a heartbeat. Thank you for gifting me a family untouched by blood and obligations.

Last but definitely not the least, Inkfeathers. My publisher and my guide, Uma Bokil. Thank you for letting me pester you for months before coming to a decision. You guys made it possible.

Thank you.

# foreword

If prose is about baring the heart, poetry is baring one's soul. And Samridhi Prakash's words are searing, visceral, piercing. In 'unbosoming', she pours herself out, as few can, as few do. Savour these lines, then, absorb them, feel them,

they stopped falling for me

the closer they came

the uglier i became

they can't understand

my mystery is messy

chaos my beauty

Eternal mystery for me: how does a youngster pen such eviscerating lines!? At an age and stage when her contemporaries must be dealing with a whole lot of issues vastly different, Samridhi shows us a glimpse of the chaos that rages within, if only we didn't mute it with Netflix and dates and such everyday stuff.

Here's more from her:

your silence so profound
your frown so deep
i trace those valleys
searching for our horizon

It was with a startle that I realised the person who penned these stark lines was all of 19. Which took me to the time when we were 19. I don't know about you, but for me it was a time when I was careening in search of a career, not knowing what to do beyond college, beyond studies. Writing, if journalism qualifies, was serendipity. In Samridhi, there's a star in the making. Her ability to dig deep and give expression to feelings, emotions and senses that we have learnt to smother, is a rare gift.

Saisuresh Sivaswamy
Journalist
Editor at Rediff.com India Ltd

## poet's message

Fair warning before you delve into my musings- it's chaotic and yet there flows the lightest of strings, piecing the story together, just like our midnight minds.

I began writing unbosoming in the late summers of 2020, with no direction, no deadline, and no inkling that these midnight thoughts would turn out to be a little something someday. Over the months, through copious phases of transition, with everyone and everything locked up inside, I wrote to escape reality and make sense of the intangible, indescribable feelings which struck at odd hours. These thoughts are unfiltered and unscripted, penned down at varying moments, in multiple headspaces, amalgamating a spectrum of overlapping emotions. None of them have headings or titles or even punctuations as these are mere thoughts, doubts, fears, insecurities, and every other emotion we hide the mirror from, in their rawest form. Each piece is unique in itself, revolving around afterthoughts that visit us at uninvited hours and refuse to depart, colonising our peace in the unseen crevices of our memories, manifesting themselves in our personality.

There is a splatter of hope in knowing that you are not alone. These poems offer no advice, nor any guidance. They are mere flawed pieces of my soul, splashed in permanent ink. The string binding it all together moves through phases of individuality, family, love, despair, hope, and ultimately the consequences, the endings. There are nights when we hate ourselves, doubt every word we speak, every thought we conjure and it was through those nights, unbosoming was born. It has my weakest and most intimate vulnerabilities wrapped in pretty letters. Today I have the courage to share this with you because now I know, it gets better. You should too.

samridhi prakash

# phases


her

them

him

destruction

reflection

echoes

her

1.

will you sit back
and read my soul for me
i have left pieces of myself
on these pages
tell me
if you could fall in love with me

2.

i forgo touch a long time back
hid it somewhere in the memories
of a four-year old's summer nap

3.

words unspoken
memories tarnished
kept against my will
bound and chained
to this pedestal of unrequited feelings
when shall i be free to leave
my palace of broken childish dreams

4.


i am afraid to write
of what my soul might bare
in the broad afternoon light with too many eyes
and no dark corner to hide

5.

i wish i had a diary of my dreams
each page a different memory
a different story
to go through my fears
to join the dots of reality and desire
from the pattern
of ghostly dreams

6.

i wrote so you could see
what feels a heart held in place by thorns
piercing through flesh
yielding support
reminding what shouldn't have been but was

7.


i stare at the lights
yellow and golden
casting shadows and doubts on my mind
laying webs of gloom
each fibre as thick and heavy as my love

8.

i see colours
they tell me i am supposed to be colour blind
but i do see colours
i feel love
they tell me i am not supposed to love
but i do love
come that day
i say i feel alive
they tell me i am not supposed to live
i will not fight

9.

happy illusions in my mental kaleidoscope
keep floating above and around
mirroring my unrealistic wishes
reflecting upon the ease with which these lies
weave stories so tempting
tying my hope into coloured knots
pretty layers covering the chaos

10.

they stopped falling for me
the closer they came
the uglier i became
they can't understand
my mystery is messy
chaos my beauty

11.

eyes are the windows to your soul
they taught me
i pulled down the blinds on mine
in love with the idea of mystery
started exploring those pretentious halls
they forgot to teach me
eyes are the vents to escape your mind
now i am too full of myself
trying to pick the locks on my slits
i had once blown away the keys to

12.

flakes of my memory
keep piecing together
distortions and lies
same place
new time
new faces
same crime
one piece of puzzle stays
imprints of your palm
in mine

## 13.

i can sense the callings
in between time
hope stretching ahead of me
distant and intangible
i am lost in those spaces
in between seconds
too tired to dream
will lie down for a while
splitting open the cracks of fate
let time wash over the remaining miles
and ponder
how must time feel
trapped in between seconds

14.

why is white the colour of loss
when i weep it's a river of chaos
no outlines
no sketches
it's murder
it's birth
there is no air
yet there is a storm
i close my eyes to see red
my vision contains black
in my sadness there sits nothing as pure as white

15.

i wish to escape
crawl under my unconscious fences
let the spikes embed in me their stories
bleed white
carving deltas across my skin
as i drown those sweet memories
in dreamy lakes of reality

16.

sing to me
trials of heaven
harps of hell
colours of loss
whispers of dark
sing to me life's arts

17.


of all the emotions hitting me
shame shamelessly stands out
this guilt is naked and raw
marrying new waves of repentance every morning
only to tip-toe away at night

18.

how should you feel when you can't feel remorse as
strongly as you should
when looking into your criminal eye becomes routine
a daily dose of black peace
when your sins string into one happy memory
a book closed and cherished
how should you feel when you can't feel human as you should

19.

it's my penance and your punishment
for my crimes
and your forgiveness

20.


i write to leave behind on these pages
a little negativity of my mind
just enough to sleep dreamlessly
and numb at night

21.

you killed the sadness in me
you killed the writer in me
she resurrects the days you are not around
spending the nights in the dim light of her laptop
clicking away at her misery

22.


i see her smile carved in sky now
i haven't seen her
yet she is the epitome of beauty
and your eyes are locked with hers
brown
unlike mine

23.

he looked at me
hushed my doubts
and said
treat yourself the way you treat me

24.


they say i am the sinner
for setting her free
but she was like that
fondling the depths of the oceanic spree
while i
shallow as the withered tree
now i have embraced her existence
sharing her breath

25.

in her eyes
the world stood still
in her eyes
the world shook still

# them

1.

she broke my heart
with her brutal honesty
biased beliefs and fallacious folklores
birthing new stories
leaving me with new experiences to write

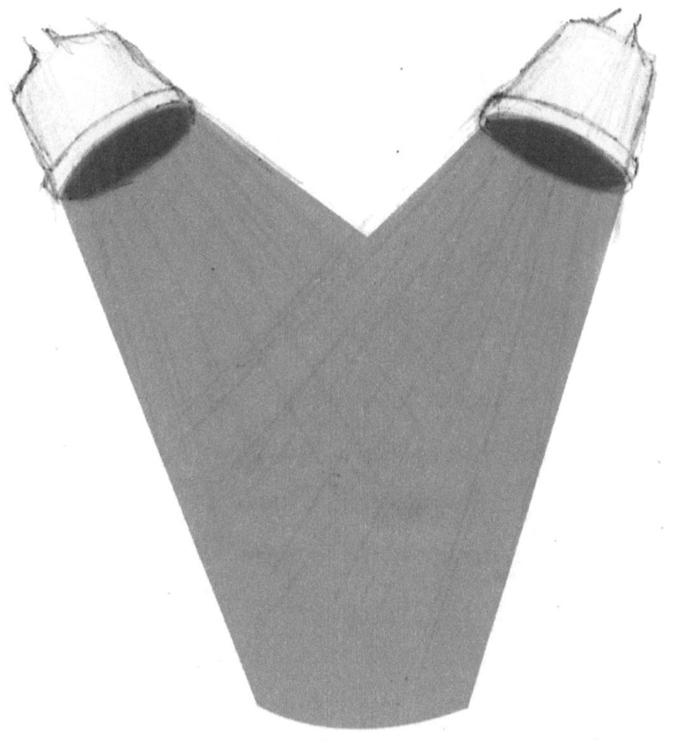

2.

i wasn't kept in the dark
worse
i was kept under fake lights

3.


and we have so many pages
with our memories splashed across
some stained in red
some as innocent as my childhood
i only want you written in bold
inked across the last page
of my life

4.


i keep waiting for you to show up
to align our stars right again
every day
only to sit back on my rocking chair
under the dim yellow lights
every night
and dream of the dreams
we were supposed to live together

5.

your silence so profound
your frown so deep
i trace those valleys
searching for our horizon

6.

i will look out for you
till our horizons blend
till your journey begins and mine ends

7.


if you die before me
leave me a list of the colours you wish to see
i will labour through each day
so you may see the phases through me

8.

when death knocks
i will follow in your footsteps ashore
let the waves sweep me away
dying sun
my only ray

9.

they were born to be
centre of my universe
and they were
after all these years i understand
why gravity exists
why the earth worships the sun
and why it's never too close
for even your protector can burn you away
from the earth i have learnt to revere
from the earth i have learnt to fear

10.

i knew you could act
you could cheat
had i only an inkling
i was the permanent resident
of your palace of deceit
i wish i had known
it was them all along
i wish i could fool myself back
into believing that laughter of our childhood was real
but how could it be
when you never were

11.

they tell me i don't know everything
but i never claimed to
i only ever said i knew you
but today you make me question my belief
the faith i hold supreme
they tell me i'm an ignorant child
dreaming in dreams

12.

you carry with yourself our family name
a family divided in love
you carry our values
but when alone you hum their tunes
i wish i knew
when the time comes whose side you would choose

13.


i don't want to doubt you
you are the basis of me
every time i have had to build myself up
you were my constant
don't let them break you
for me

14.

interwoven
intertwined
they ran parallel
her destiny's course and mine

15.


i feel distant
your hours of silence haunt my seconds
your laughter is heard
echoing
in hallways parallel to mine
i see you
unseeing me

16.


i can see your happiness
screaming at me through these photographs
i should be happy
but oh you are so happy without me
while i fight for you in dreams

17.

you are always out
on roads
across seas
with neighbours and enemies
tying knots and mending ties
and i stand inside
on broken glass
screaming
bleeding
but you don't hear me
in the din of the spotlight
when you visit home
it is to build fences so high
my liberty
wrapped
caresses the sky
and i kneel inside
on flooded floors

weeping
soaking
but you don't see me
in the chorus of the popularity
answer my fear once
after all is done
the neighbours know you by your name
the perimeters are secure
will you come back home

18.

how could you not tell me
it wasn't the same for you
after all these months you pull away
overconscious of your actions
of what might my parents say
for me
it has been about us not them
how could i not see
you were never interested in me

19.

you keep trying to make amends
but how can i tell you
it won't ever be the same
how can i trust you again
i look into your eyes
watching remnant distrust unfold
laughing me at my face
for being so naive
let me not look in your eyes again

20.


you made me feel special
for a long time
for all the wrong reasons

21.

my curse has been to love you
unconditionally
now even if you bind me in your chains
i cannot help but keep loving you

22.

how could i not respect the being you are
eccentric and sensitive at heart
for you to doubt my love after all these years
shows how little you showed yourself to me then
how little you think of me now

23.

i wish i could show you
colours i hide beneath
skins i wear underneath
the one you are proud of

24.


i don't feel beautiful
and you are not there
to make me

25.

will you rest my head in your lap tonight
my thoughts are running wild
play with my hair
and massage my eyes
sing to me lores from your childhood
so i might forget mine
just one night

26.

i fear the day you will read my words
your eyes might lose their shine
your eyes might never look into mine
i'll be myself in the truest shades
as you witness an outsider

27.

all generations have their own travails
we can't go through what you had to
you can't go through what we do
we don't live in your scarred yesterdays
we exist in the limbo that is today
labouring to survive through to morrow
i respect the way you have walked
admire the path you have carved
but remember this is not your yesterday
it's my tomorrow

28.


you killed my trees and plants
my past i had sown within
you uprooted my memories in your play
you made my flowers cry
you took my chance at a different ending away

29.

i have looked up to you all my life
don't let me know now
your light was a mere reflection
my eyes are accustomed to your ethereal shine
illuminating my dreams
don't fracture my way of life

30.

you have held my hair
as i have drowned myself in misery
stepping ahead of me when my fears whispered at night
looking behind to ensure i had my shoes on tight
don't
don't walk away now
i never knew
one day there would be no you

31.

you will miss him
while sitting in his favourite corner
there will be no escape
your pain will never fade
the wound will always be raw
but his memory will make you wiser

32.

if i could paint
you would be my canvas
pink and gold
fresh meadow pastel covers
rock your core

33.

i was written in phases
some intricate and divine
some verses lost in time
but you
you have been the never-ending music of my life

34.

and a morning shall come
when it won't be in their eyes
you will search for grace
but your own

him

1.

i met him on a sunday morning
caffeine coursing through our souls
our cups clinked
eyes met
this brain screamed catastrophe
but oh this heart
blindly paraded on that tightrope

2.

this is new for me
for years now i haven't chased one
used to people chasing me
i need time to get used to this anomaly

3.


your fingers stretch twice as long as mine
i wonder what it would feel like
to have them stroke my waistline
one step closer to sin
crossing over to my heaven

4.

there is something prepossessing about him
his voice and ever-present confidence
building me up
roots growing in places unknown
fulfilling my ravenous hunger
he feeds my soul

5.

should i call you my home
all warmth and sweetness
your tender lips whispering worries away
sketching through my life a golden ray
can you not see it branded across my eyes
i long to belong

6.

he plays with the harps
i hide in the dungeons of my heart
gently pulling at the weaker strings
counting the regret-dipped memoirs i keep
healing the memories which still bleed

7.

you water the skins of sky
as i carve across them our fate
you see us in shades
as i pen our tale in phases

8.

lying together on the damp grass
hands touching and feet apart
the rug curling over the edges
trees standing guard
this was our moment
you kept staring into my eyes
while i worshipped my stars

9.

even the dust you showed me
feels like the remains of stars
a part of you glowing in every crevice
of this death marred town
speaks to me in a language
not known to any world
but our own

10.

you gave me hope
to end an era of aridness
planting peonies in my wildest dreams
but did the vendor not teach you
they need constant care
caring touch
touching reassurance
you come and go as you please
watering my dead dreams

11.

there's a new fire behind those eyes
a new sensation in that touch
after all these years
and i wonder if my time's up
if it's still me you love

12.

you stood before me
forsaking my affection
my attachment
our fate turned blue
falling backward in time
memory flashes replacing phosphenes
the strings of hope holding me up
lost faith in me

13.


i am blinded by your beauty
somedays i know it's mine
somedays when you are not around
i realise others must be too

14.


i changed my habits for you
and you came oh so close after so long
letting me touch you
keeping your hands away
i crave for your attention
but you have had this before
girls walking in every door
as you sit and bathe in your godly glow
dipped in sin and dripping with honey

## 15.

you say it's me and it will be
but our story is scrapped across
the dried-up walls of forgotten caves
while it's her name
bathed in bold
adorning the front page

16.


and though you walk beside me
i can't seem to shake off
dreams which altered my vision last night
i see you with her
and your hands fit perfectly

17.

what if you remember her scent
the way her hair cascaded across your pretty face
what if you miss her touch
the way she serenely paraded her pretty body around
what if she still lives in your dreams
as i breathe my future with you

18.


was it her hair
was it her voice
was it her fetching eyes
her beauty hurts to look at
my reality hurts to look at

19.

i can see her long hair
her protective arms wrapped around you
oh you look alive
you look distant
i mess around in the shadows
waiting for your acknowledgment
to paint me a smile

20.

you shared yourself with her
open and free
you experienced your firsts with her
shouldn't it have been me
why did you hide yourself from me
i could have loved you easily

21.


i fell in love not with your looks
but your lies
slowly
loving you became a lie

22.

you led me on once
and look how badly i clung to you
you try to pull away now
but my dreams don't give up
holding on to every word you spare at hours
tracing new stories
stitching old scars

## 23.

you took from me my pride when you walked away
i stood in the rain
my camisole sodden
silent
serene
sobbing
that last shred of dignity
being dragged down the road

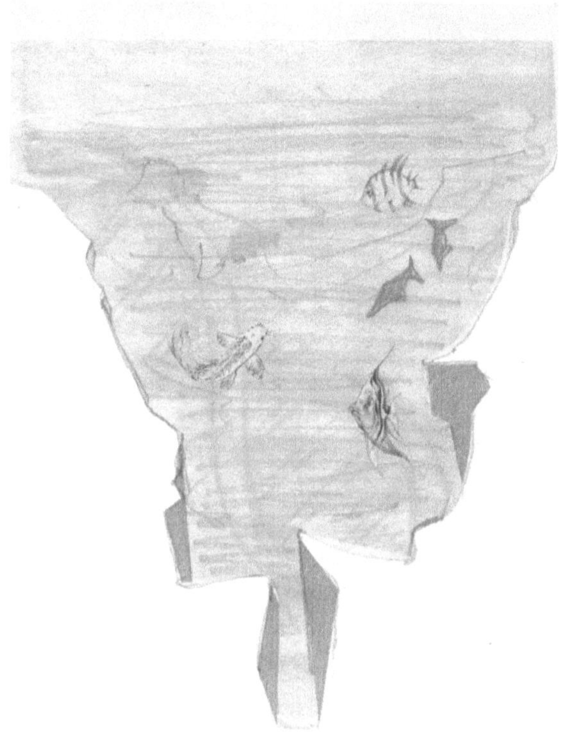

24.

i see myself brighter in your light
sinking in your love by dusk
burning myself out by night
i see myself smaller in your light
stretching towards the ocean bed
searching for my own light

25.

this morning feels stretched
straining against melancholy
pumping veins with misery
blink once so i may sense you
or else
this shroud of sadness may subsume in eternity

26.

sleep comes with your voice
dripping love inside my soul
adrenaline rush in dreams
leaving this abode lifeless
nights i sleep alone

27.

whispers of my name echo
in the hallways of your heart
deep into the silent night
dying down the moment
she steps into the sunlight
rays caught in her brows
hair curling at her nape
she lives the life i fake

28.

all these years i spent hating her
and not you
but today i realize
you meant not to hurt me
you meant to choose her
i was a mere casualty
the variable we all forgot about

29.

it's been years since you chose her
yet that a smirk sets my heart ablaze
memories smell of smoke
yet lips speak of animal desire
i see regret behind those lying eyes
yet i walk away

30.

in the forgotten world
fire and ferns fenced us
it rained incessantly
bed wasn't warm
lights not bright
had you been there
that inferno would have been ether

31.

i wish i could write you love poems again
but something inside me has snapped
permanently
maybe the threads connecting my heart to my brain

32.

i wait for that click all day long
instantly rushing over
to lay bare my soul
for your heavenly abode
you are gentle but never too close
why can't i see
you will never wait for me

33.

you have opened my eyes
making me see you in a new light
don't blame me now
for a change in perspective
it was you who made me see through your lies

34.

she spoke not with her words
but her eyes
days spent in sparkling mischief
nights followed with hollow cries

35.

it wasn't about who you were
rather who i could have been
so i broke your heart
to take back my own
weaving a path
to be traversed alone

36.

you came back
a fist of wistful fantasy
following your wake
i dreamt of waking up
living those fantasies
but now
i only allow myself
to dream of you in my dreams

37.

i feel for you not in seasons
but in moods
hate lasts long
love
love's long gone

# destruction

1.

fold me away in your arms
somewhere the world will never see
break me to shards
something the world will never touch

2.

i begged my brain to stop last night
stop sending me vivid images
of girls swooning over you
dancing with you
touching you

3.

i cling to you like death
that old vine gripping your soul
walking a yard ahead
dancing with your shadows
while you sleep to death

4.

heard his footsteps recede and fall
sinking down the grainy wall
i scooted on the bathroom floor
naked and torn
still wishing for my abuser to turn around
and pick me up
pick my million pieces of dignity
to glue us back together
and be my hero again

5.


i paint fitting outlines on my canvas
filled with my favourite hues
to label you
its only after some time
your true colours start seeping in
smudging my dream art
as i do it all over again
a new outline and my favourite parts

6.

if only you had stayed
i could have shaped you a little more
a little to the right
a sprinkle of gold
you could have fit my perfect mould

7.

now the mirror screams at me alone
his ghostly hands rule my waist no more
i should be happy
but this bed feels so cold

8.

oh they were right again
forever is for fantasies
and my childish dreams

9.

i slapped my face black
ecstasy flowering my soul
blame
misery and pity
rushed in at once
i had never felt more at home

10.

i don't feel respected
in my own eyes
my questionable choices
and porous lies

11.


i cannot see you begin
but i live my life
fathoming your end
aligning it to fit the angles
of my existence

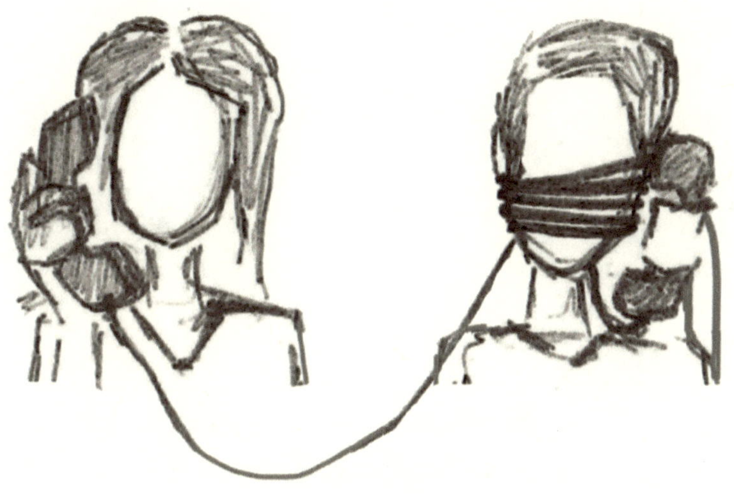

12.

i missed a word or few
a hundred times
i held on too tight
my breath
making you hold your own

13.


self-mockery follows your calls
reflections in every whisper
its branded in bold
my permanent badge of failure

14.

i died today
she died today
you died today
we all say goodbye every day
die a little every day

## 15.

can't remember the last night i had the luxury of dreaming
a sub-conscious truth toying away with reality
a little dark
a little dirty
place in my dreams
something terrible
haunting
a nightmare if that's what it takes to make me feel
but darling fairy
just come and bestow upon me a dream

16.

the glow of the unborn truth
staining the sky in a reddish hue
or is it the dying one
red is everywhere
the ultimate truth
death is coming
omega will be fulfilling

17.

tripping on my mental rocks
bleeding
i can feel the spiral forming
mist is here
calling upon the elements
and in my mind my shadow hides
scared where these thoughts might lead
i grow quieter
retreating in my shell
as the storm intensifies
and my feet paint those downward roads red
walking paths i could sketch in death

18.

night sings of glory
shrieks of pain
sky's beloved glow hangs low
in the darkest hole of my mind
insanity grows

19.


my words travel through heavy air
your wisdom claws at them
dissecting their soul
what remains is worth nothing
as if it began worth something

20.

i can see you trying
reaching for me
how do i tell you
i can't feel my fingers no more
blood drips through
let me see again
let me feel again
help me then

21.

keep your comfort close
your pity closer
and let me hate myself
in peace

22.


you should walk away
for i am no one
you would want by your side
i myself push my shadow away

23.

unseen spaces scream
when you show me my mistakes
my way of life is flawed
i thrive in denial
and breathe in deceit

24.


will you sketch me
i'll leave a blank cheque by the lamp
paint me thin eyebrows
sharper eyes
high cheekbones
fuller lips
paint a better life

25.


every day i feel closer to lighting my own pyre
sitting atop those woods
hungry and delirious
feeding on fire

26.

she was a little broken
so i broke her more
now piecing her back together
more to my taste than before

27.

look at me so i can get through this
your eyes hold the better me
it's been a month and i expect fealty
look at me so i don't turn to memories
to hold me

reflection

1.

and i wonder what's better

having it then losing all

or

having none and not losing at all

2.

my arguments have no logic
nor any reason
it's all coated in emotion
the strand no one bothers about

3.

oh but how do i smile
i don't know what hurts
where it hurts
numbness floats inside my head
an eerie calm
fogging my mind
bright lights blind every corner
every speck of pain spinning starkly
draining fear

4.

the worst isn't not knowing your worth
in their life
the worst is being misled into believing
you are worth more
than anyone they have known

5.

i questioned the way i surrendered to you
in those lonely nights
when i couldn't sleep without you
i roamed the house at 4 am
bare feet
sat on the balcony swing
feeling the windless atmosphere
i couldn't breathe
i wondered if love should feel that lonely

6.

and when family inflicts upon family
flesh heals
it's the threads binding the home
which keep tricking the soul

7.

how does one react
when they tell you your home isn't built deep
bricks adulterated with sand
and there is a pit underneath
carved in the downward spiral of time
and those memories you so ardently worship
are wisps of lie
spun so beautifully in the fabric of time
you are forever trapped inside

8.

and how you scream at others
for feelings intangible in your eyes
believing the half-truths
trading even them for lies
and how i scream at others
for feelings tangible in my life
reflecting on memories
trying to trade them for lies

9.

is there anyone you are afraid to look into the eye
for they have known too much of you
they might piece you back together
make you remember
you were better
a lifetime ago

10.

i am a kid
with fake accolades
earning years of pitiful consolation
stuffing myself with hollow pride

11.

i feel every day
i feel enough
some days the words dry up
making me feel i don't feel enough

12.

i sense the existence of my past self
in the mirrors i pass by
in shards she lingers
their brave
melancholy whispers

echoes

**him.**

after the bliss was over
i could see we were not the same
but you were worth my efforts and time
so i stayed on to make you mine
it never dawned upon me
you could hurt me so casually.

**them.**

you will always be a part of me
i will love you from my distance
with this sea fuming between us
neither shall cross over
neither shall stop looking for the other.

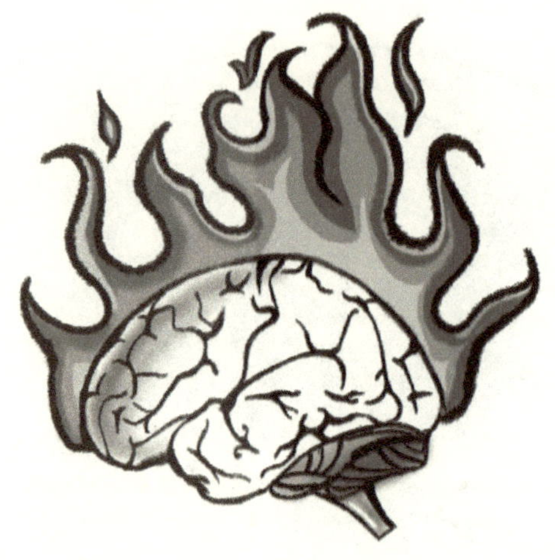

**destruction.**

i cannot explain this
it doesn't make sense to me
it hurts deep in my chest cavity
pinching thoughts in a whirlwind
grinding against rationality
all i know is
it hurts incessantly.

**her.**

all my life i have lived in shadows
all my life i have loved in shadows
don't ask me to step into the light
i know not how to breathe
if not in life's shadows

a voice speaks to me inside my head
not to heed whatever's coming next
it bellows
it grinds
breathing with the mystery of time.

# about the author

Raised in the city of Delhi, Samridhi aced academics in school and is currently pursuing BA LLB from Symbiosis Law School. A Nritya Visharad (Bachelor's) in Odissi, she has performed in various dance festivals across India and the globe.

Samridhi can be found glued to her desk, fervently jotting down text at the back of her notebook. When not lost in her world, Samridhi can be found cooking, reading, putting things back at their places, swooning over Halsey's & TS's lyrics, worrying about her CV, or fangirling over "The Office". Afterall,

"There is a lot of beauty in ordinary things, isn't that kind of the point?"

# INKFEATHERS PUBLISHING

*India's Most Author Friendly Publishing House*

Stay updated about the latest books, anthologies, events, exclusive offers, contests, product giveaways and other things that we do to support authors.

 Inkfeathers Publishing

 @InkfeathersPublishing

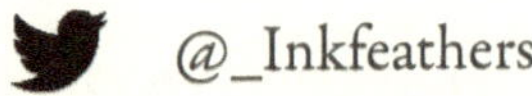 @_Inkfeathers

 @Inkfeathers

 Inkfeathers.com

*We'd love to connect with you!*